GOOD GRIEF

GIFT EDITION

GOOD GRIEF

A COMPANION FOR EVERY LOSS

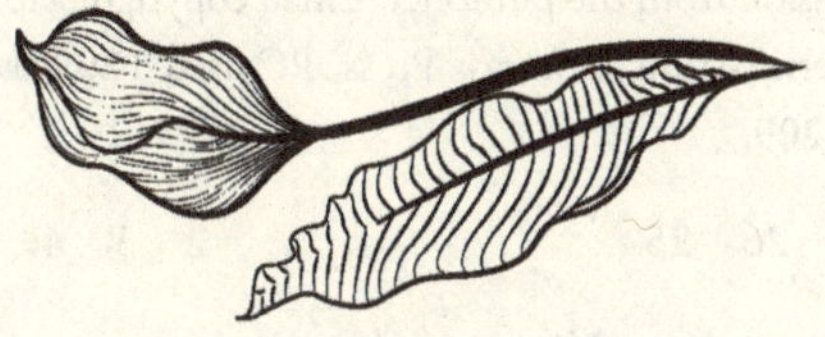

GRANGER E. WESTBERG

Foreword by Dr. Timothy Johnson, MD

Devotions by Brent D. Christianson

Fortress Press
Minneapolis

GOOD GRIEF GIFT EDITION
A Companion for Every Loss

29 28 27 26 25 2 3 4 5 6 7 8 9

Reflection questions provided and additional Scripture passages selected by the Rev. Sally L. Wilke.

Cover design: Fortress Press
Cover image: © 2025 Getty Images; Peace lily flowers hand draw/1172218216 by lumyaisweet

Print ISBN: 979-8-8898-3691-9
eBook ISBN: 979-8-8898-3803-6

To the memory of my sister Viola,
who helped so many find hope in the midst of grief

CONTENTS

FOREWORD

I HAD THE great pleasure of getting to know Granger Westberg personally and professionally during my year of study at the University of Chicago Divinity School in 1960–61. He was on the faculty of both the medical center and the divinity school. I was struggling with my faith journey as it was being vigorously challenged by the intense intellectual atmosphere of the divinity school. My struggle was both physically and spiritually upsetting. In retrospect I realize I was grieving the loss of my simple childhood faith.

So I sought out the counsel of this pioneer in the chaplaincy movement. His gentle physical presence, kind smile, and soothing voice were immediately therapeutic. And his insights about the nature of my struggle—and his reassurance about the normalcy of what I was experiencing—were more effective than any pill could possibly have been. Our dialogue that year became the basis for a lifelong friendship.

At about the same time, Granger wrote a short book encapsulating his vast experience with the many faces of grieving he had encountered in his work as a pastor, chaplain, and teacher. It was tantalizingly titled *Good Grief* and quickly became a best seller, with total sales to date of about three million copies! Its popularity is due in part to the fact that it talks openly about all kinds of grief, from loss through death to loss from divorce, being fired, moving, and struggles with children.

I just finished rereading this gem. It is immediately clear why it has been and will continue to be a best seller. It is written with the heart of a pastor, the insight of a psychologist, the humanity of a father and husband, and the hope of someone who has seen so many survive the process of grieving. It is simple but not simplistic. It is profound but not professorial. Most importantly, it describes the pathway through grieving that can only be found through honesty. This is a book that should be in the hands of anyone grieving for any reason.

Dr. Timothy Johnson, MD
2011

PREFACE

I AM DEEPLY grateful that so many of you have found this little book helpful in your experience of grief.

I have learned during these many years that the various forms of loss that come our way need not be entirely damaging; they can, to some degree at least, also be life-enhancing. Suffering is not good, but you need not be devastated by it. Ultimately we can be healed of our bitterness and move ahead.

And so what can be the result of reading this book of good grieving?

- We come out of our grief experience at a slightly higher level of maturity than before.
- We come out of our grief as deeper persons because we have been down in the depths of despair and know what it is like.
- We come out of it stronger, for we have had to learn how to use our spiritual muscles to climb the rugged mountain trails.

- We come out of it better able to help others. We have walked through the valley of the shadow of grief. We can understand.

That is why I have chosen to call this little book *Good Grief.*

Granger E. Westberg

INTRODUCTION

WE SPEND A good portion of our lives working diligently to acquire those things that make life rich and meaningful—friends, a wife or husband, children, a home, a job, material comforts, money (let's face it), and security. What happens to us when we lose any of these persons or things that are so important to us?

Quite naturally we grieve over the loss of anything important. Sometimes, if the loss is great, the very foundations of our life are shaken, and we are thrown into deep despair. Because we know so little about the nature of grief, we become panicky when it strikes us, and this serves to throw us deeper into despondency. What can we learn about the "grief process" so that we can better cope with it?

Does people's faith have anything to do with the way they grieve over whatever it is they lose? For instance, when we lose a job, or lose a loving friend, or fail in school, or are disliked by the people at the office because of our unpopular convictions, does our grief at these times have anything to do with our faith?

Faith plays a major role in grief of any kind. But not in the way some people think. They often seem to have the idea that a person with strong faith does not grieve and is above this sort of thing. Moreover, these people imply that religious faith advocates stoicism. They might even quote the two words from Scripture "Grieve not!" They forget to quote the rest of the phrase in which these two words are found: "Grieve not as those who have no hope" (1 Thessalonians 4:13).

But religious faith—at least the Jewish-Christian faith—has never said that a truly religious person does not grieve. What it has said is that there are good ways and bad ways to grieve and that what a person considers to be of most importance in life will definitely affect the way he or she grieves.

The theme of this book is "good grief" because we will try to explore the good aspects of grief. We will try to describe not only the pattern of grief but also what we can learn from it. And since everyone in a lifetime must, from time to time, confront the loss of something or someone he or she loves, this booklet is for everyone.

If we include our "little griefs" along with our "large griefs," we can say that grief is as natural to every person as breathing. It is inevitable! You cannot live without experiencing it in a thousand different ways. Such a seemingly inconsequential thing as your husband phoning at the last minute, just before guests are arriving for dinner, to say that he has to work late throws you into a mild form of grief. Or perhaps the boss under whom you have worked happily for ten years is suddenly transferred, and the new one is pompous and overbearing. This is a form of grief. How you handle these "little griefs" will, in some measure, tell you how you will probably handle the larger griefs when they come.

It is now possible to predict fairly well some of the things that will happen to all of us when something or someone very essential to our particular way of life is taken away. Before we describe the pattern that most of us follow, however, let us be sure we can picture grief in several more forms. We certainly mean to include grief related to death in this discussion, but we can observe the same grief process at work in many other kinds of losses as well.

For instance, one of the more common grief situations arises out of our mobile culture. In America, one out of five people moves every year because of change of employment or promotion. The uprooting of families on the American scene has been going on long enough for us to be able to identify certain forms of emotional instability that result from it. The uprooted family is cut off from stabilizing relationships in the community that every child and adult needs so much. Every member of the family is adversely affected as they are pulled away from people and things that have grown dear to them.

There is every reason to raise the question whether corporations that transfer their key employees every two to five years are doing a wise thing, either for the family or ultimately for industry itself.

Let us look at a particular family that has been transferred three times in several years. They have lived in the present town for two years, and their children, after some difficulty, finally feel comfortable with their playmates and at school. The company now "invites" the father to move for the fourth time. The mother in this family says that they have never before felt such a sense of belonging as they have in their present town. They had hoped they could stay there a long time. But her husband is on his way to a vice-presidency, and the corporation operates on the assumption that it is good for its executives to move frequently.

In the light of our new knowledge of psychosomatic medicine, we are not so sure it is a good idea. We who have spent years teaching in hospitals and medical centers see a great many sick or upset people who have come into the hospital during such an uprooting experience. I have seen children who are thrown into turmoil three months before the move and for three months or more after the move.

Certainly such practices contribute to the instability of our society, and business institutions would do well to take a second look at the long-term results of such constant moving.

Or think of the problem of divorce. Certainly divorce is a situation that creates grief in the hearts of those who have now lost someone who once was dear to them. It is almost like a living death to see the one whom you continue to love turning his or her back on you, figuratively slapping you in the face.

Another form of grief may be retirement. Not all people look forward to retirement at any age. They feel that they are good for at least another ten years. But then time and circumstances may make retirement necessary, in spite of their wishes. And many of these people leave their jobs with heavy hearts.

We think of grief in relation to a man in his forties who is laid off indefinitely because of a business recession.

Then there is the person who has worked diligently to gain advancement, who has worked overtime and weekends to demonstrate ability to fill a particular position. After several years that job is finally open, and he is sure he will be chosen. But the boss remembers he has a nephew who needs a job, and the nephew takes over. Is this a cause for grief? Of course it is!

Another grief situation may center around the children of a family. A child is lost not through death but through marriage. He takes all his belongings from his room, and the house is lifeless. A house once filled with laughter and joy is now as quiet as a tomb. Or another child may turn against her mother and father and live her life in a manner completely contrary to their teachings. Or perhaps a college-age son or daughter who is deeply in love and making plans for marriage discovers his or her future mate has been untrue, and the wedding plans must be canceled.

A list of losses would be inexhaustible. We can lose our health, our eyesight, our hearing. We can lose our home through fire or tornado or financial ruin. In some families, grief comes with the loss of a pet that has been a part of everything that has gone on in that household for ten years or more. Any of these things, and many more, can set in motion a cycle of grief.

Grief is a natural part of human experience. We face minor grief almost daily in some situation or another.

To say a person is deeply religious and therefore does not have to face grief situations is ridiculous. Not only is it totally unrealistic, but it is also incompatible with the whole Christian message.

The one Bible verse every Sunday school child knows by heart is the two-word verse "Jesus wept." These words describe a man who, when grief came, was able to weep, for he wanted and needed to express the feelings within him.

When we say, "Grieve not," then we imply we are to be Stoics like the Greeks of old. But we do not subscribe to the philosophy of the Stoics. Christians should know the difference between Stoicism and Christianity. The Scriptures, both Old and New Testaments, see grief as normal and potentially creative.

I suggest that in this eight-word portion of Scripture we put a comma after the first word so that it now reads, "Grieve, not as those who have no hope," and then I would add "but for goodness' sake, grieve when you have something worth grieving about!"

We ministers discovered some years ago that many of the people we counseled were suffering from some form of sorrow they had not as yet been able to work through. As we began to try to understand the problems of our parishioners in distress, we sensed they were reacting to the loss of some precious relationship or possession in much the same way people react to the loss of a loved one through death.

We also began to sense that people in sorrow—from whatever cause—tend to follow a pattern that includes several stages.

The idea of stages of grief was first suggested to us by Dr. Erich Lindemann, professor of psychiatry at Harvard, who described the grief process in an article titled "Symptomology and Management of Acute Grief," published in *The American Journal of Psychiatry* years ago.

In this remarkable study, he demonstrated the difference between normal grief reactions and abnormal or morbid grief. He showed the importance of helping the grief-stricken person face up to the struggle of "working through" grief. The person has to be helped to "extricate himself from the bondage to the deceased and find new patterns of rewarding interaction."

Dr. Lindemann then described five things he saw in acute grief: (1) somatic distress, (2) preoccupation with the image of the deceased, (3) guilt, (4) hostile reactions, and (5) loss of patterns of conduct.

Dr. Lindemann's studies encouraged clergymen to deal more objectively with grief reactions in their parishioners. They soon found that parishioners who faced up to their loss by wrestling openly and honestly with the problem came through the grieving experience stronger, deeper, and better able to help other people with their grieving.

Of course, this wrestling with problems connected with loss also caused the parishioner to reevaluate her own religious convictions. This meant that the parishioner began to question aspects of her faith and often went through periods of doubt in which she questioned the relevance of the Christian faith to personal problems. If, however, she was able to maintain some kind of relationship with God through regular worship and through fellowship with people of the congregation who really cared about her, then she looked upon the struggle as a growth experience that actually deepened her faith. Like Job of old, she was beset on all sides, but she refused to give up her basic faith.

Through the centuries, people who have been able to face grief in the knowledge that God still cares about them have said that grief can be counted among the great deepening experiences of life.

The ten stages of grief described here must be understood to be the normal process through which most people must go as they face up to their loss. In other words, we will be talking about the road the majority of humans must travel in order to get back into the mainstream of life.

As we look at these ten stages of grief, remember that every person does not necessarily go through all these stages, nor in this order. Moreover, it is impossible to differentiate clearly between each of these stages, for a person never moves neatly from one stage to the other.

But you, O Lord, are a shield around me,
my glory, and the one who lifts up my head.
I cry aloud to the Lord,
and he answers me from his holy hill.

—Psalm 3:3–4

STAGE 1

We Are in a State of Shock

STAGE ONE

We Are in a State of Shock

GOD HAS SO made us that we can somehow bear pain and sorrow and even tragedy. However, when the sorrow is overwhelming, we are sometimes temporarily anesthetized in response to a tragic experience. We are grateful for this temporary anesthesia, for it keeps us from having to face grim reality all at once. This shock stage—or perhaps it should be called a countershock—may last anywhere from a few minutes to a few hours to a few days. If it goes on for some weeks, it probably is unhealthy grief and professional help ought to be sought.

But do not be afraid of the shock that often comes in the early stages of grief. Sometimes at the funeral home we see the sorrowing wife and find that she is almost radiant as she greets those who have come to offer their sympathy. People say, "What serene faith she has!" We tend to equate faith with a stoical attitude, not with tears. Yet, the truth of the matter may well be that this woman is experiencing a temporary anesthesia that is helping her along until she is ready to move on to the next stage of grief.

We tend to equate faith with a stoical attitude, not with tears.

The minister, upon seeing this woman in what at least appears to be shock, will arrange to visit her after the funeral, knowing that one day soon this strong exterior may break down, and he will have to help her face her true self. In fact, in some cases he may even encourage her to break down and express openly the strong emotions she was not able to admit earlier.

A man who was unexpectedly fired from a job he had held for twenty years put it this way: "I was so stunned by what they told me, I walked around as if I was in a trance. What they said just did not register. I heard the words, but they had not 'reached' me yet."

Shock is a temporary escape from reality. As long as it is temporary, it is good. But if a person should prefer to remain in this dreamworld rather than face the reality of his loss, obviously it would be very unhealthy.

This is one of the reasons it is good for us to keep fairly busy and continue to carry on as much of our usual activities as possible during the period of crisis. It is certainly not good to have someone take over completely for us at such a time and make all our decisions for us.

Well-meaning relatives and friends might hinder the grief process by forcing us to sit inactively by. This would be much like the surgery patients in the past who were coddled and told not to do anything, not even turn over in bed for several days after surgery. All of this had the effect of making the patient sicker, and it required a much longer period for him to make his comeback.

The same thing is true with grief. The sooner the person has to deal with the immediate problems and make decisions again, the better.

The housemother of a large sorority house at a midwestern university says of her many experiences with girls who "receive bad news from home": "I always make it a point to be right there near the girl the whole time she is making telephone calls and preparing to leave. But I always keep her as busy as I can, letting her do her own packing and making her own minute-to-minute decisions. The other girls in the house always want to wait on her hand and foot, but I've learned that this is the worst thing you can do for a person at such a time."

To sum up: Be near the person and available to help if everything breaks down, but normally do not take away from him the therapeutic value of doing everything he can for himself. This is what will help a person most to come out of his trance and "get on with his grief work," as Erich Lindemann might say.

Even though a person does come out of the initial shock, he will undoubtedly experience times in the succeeding days and months when the unreality of the loss comes over him again. Every now and then he will say, "I just can't believe it has happened. Intellectually I know it did, but I guess I just have not really accepted it emotionally."

The biggest hurdle is "accepting it emotionally."

For all of us, the biggest hurdle is "accepting it emotionally." We just do not want to believe it, and so unconsciously we set as many barriers in the way as possible, making complete acceptance a very slow process.

Although you want to avoid making major decisions, what decisions are you able to make that could restore a sense of reality? In the midst of loss, it may seem everything has been uprooted. What are the anchors you are able to take hold of now? Are you able to identify the barriers that keep you in a state of disbelief? How could you address them?

DEVOTIONAL

Draw Near, O Love: Shock and God

The Christian faith proclaims the presence and activity of God to be consistent and clear. But many people have felt themselves witnesses to God's silence, the sense of God's absence or indifference, and have expressed frustration or doubt about God's nearness. That feeling about God is not rare or unusual.

When we grieve and are in the stage of shock, the disruption we experience is not only internal or with people and the world around us. That disruption can also appear in our relationship with God. While our primary relationship might be with ourselves, our most important relationship is with God.

The cry of desertion we may feel echoes the words of Jesus himself on the cross "My God, my God, why have you forsaken me?" (Matthew 27:46). He felt God's silence.

When, in our grief and pain, we question not only the love of God but the very existence of God, those around us may react with their own shock and worry about our souls. What they perceive as our doubt may also summon up uncomfortable feelings for them about their own faith.

We try to keep in mind that if God the Father can put up with such thoughts from God the Son, God can certainly handle our own shocked and challenged faith. I used to tell couples who were preparing to marry to learn how to "fight fairly." I suggested that if there were no disagreements, they might not be taking the relationship seriously.

To bring such doubts, such challenges, such a "fight" to God is not a sign of lack of faith but a sign that we take that relationship with God seriously enough not to be afraid to contend.

When we question God, wonder about God, even doubt God, it is good for us to remember the adage that the opposite of love is not hate but indifference. We are dealing with a relationship of ultimate importance during a highly difficult time in our lives.

We don't give up the dialogue. In this relationship, as with others, it is wise and healthy not to turn our backs on what had been our normal activity.

Have you always prayed or taken time for devotional reading or meditation? Try to continue that practice, but in your prayers, seek to be honest about your thoughts and feelings. God knows them already, but it is good for us to hear ourselves saying those things.

Worship may have always been a part of your life. For some people, it is hard to return to the worshiping community. Returning with a friend or family member often eases the process.

In this stage of grief, things are off kilter. But through all of this, the hope and the promise we have is that when the shock diminishes we will find that God is with us as God has always been, loving us and holding us.

To Think About

Have you experienced other times in your life when God seemed distant or silent? Think about how that felt to you. What words describe that feeling?

To Talk About

Find a good friend, a clergyperson, or a spiritual director and talk about your current relationship with God, your ability to feel God's presence, your desire to feel it, whether you are able to pray or worship. Talk about how your relationship to God feels.

To Do

If worship, prayer, devotional reading, or meditation have been a part of your life but you have stopped those practices, choose one of these activities and set a specific time when you will begin to step back into it. Write it down and note when you have carried it out.

Prayer

God, I'm not sure I want to talk to you now. I need you to help me know that you have not deserted me, that you hear me, that you see me, and that you are with me. I think you know how I feel. Help me to know how you love. Amen.

How long, O Lord? Will you forget me forever?
How long will you hide your face from me?
How long must I bear pain in my soul,
and have sorrow in my heart all day long?
—Psalm 13:1–2

STAGE

We Express Emotion

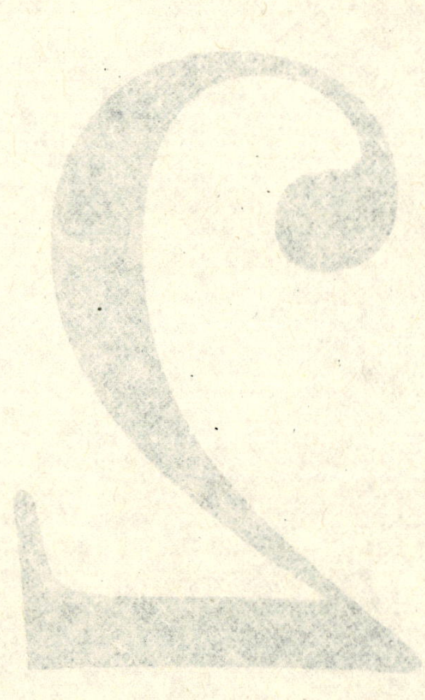

STAGE TWO

We Express Emotion

EMOTIONAL RELEASE COMES at about the time it begins to dawn upon us how dreadful this loss is. Sometimes without warning there wells up within us an uncontrollable urge to express our grief. And this is exactly what we ought to do: allow ourselves to express the emotions we actually feel. We have been given tear glands, and we are supposed to use them when we have good reason to use them.

And this is exactly what we ought to do: allow ourselves to express the emotions we actually feel.

In our society it is very difficult for men to cry, because they have been taught as little tots that boys do not cry. When a little boy falls and skins his knee and cries out in fright and pain, someone picks him up and says, "Now, now, little man, don't cry!" And when he is eight years old and hurts himself, he does not dare to cry, nor at eighteen when something happens about which he ought to cry. At thirty-eight when some great loss is suffered, he cannot cry.

Many men think that not only is crying a sign of weakness but that letting themselves go emotionally might lead to a nervous breakdown. This has been disproven for years, yet men seem not to understand that it is the person who holds himself tense, who refuses to let go, who may be in for trouble. The Scriptures clearly show that when great calamities came to the hardy men of faith, they wept bitterly; their "tears were with them all the night long."

When we speak about emotional release, it reminds us of the whole subject of emotions and our faith. Are we saying that religion should advocate emotionalism? No, but neither are we in favor of an emotion*less* religion. Emotion is essential to a person, and to try to repress it is to make one less than a person.

Emotion is essential to a person, and to try to repress it is to make one less than a person.

For us to imagine we can live fully and deeply without emotion is pretty ridiculous. We are not talking now about emotionalism. We are talking about the emotions that provide the motivation for everything we do.

One of the great faults of intellectual Protestantism is that it has tended to stifle emotion. The Sunday services have more resembled a lecture series than a worship experience. We must not and need not apologize for emotion in our religious experience, nor need we apologize for it in our grief.

To bottle it up unnecessarily is to do ourselves harm. We ought to express the grief we feel. Some will be too embarrassed to grieve openly; they can go off by themselves and let their grief take its natural course in any of a variety of ways.

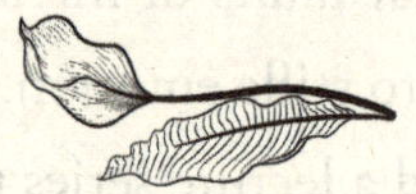

What did you learn as a child about expressing emotion? How is that helpful or not helpful to you now? Who are the people who may help you express your feelings?

DEVOTIONAL

Being Emotionally Honest

After this Job opened his mouth and cursed the day of his birth. Job said:

"Let the day perish on which I was born,
and the night that said,
'A man-child is conceived.'"

—Job 3:1–3

The book of Job is powerful for many reasons. One thing it teaches us is how not to react to a friend's expression of emotion. Job is afflicted in many ways; his friends come to be with him. They maintain silence until Job begins his lament, his expression of deep emotions. Rather than listening to him, they try to correct him, and most of the rest of the book is Job expressing emotion and his friends increasingly denying his right to do so.

With grief comes a flood of emotions. When we are able to put a finger on what the emotions are, we will find great healing in sharing those emotions with others.

Some people, like Job's friends, will find themselves frightened by our emotions, downplay them, or caution us to suppress or deny what we are feeling. This response may hurt us (and that hurt may lead to anger), so we do need to keep in mind that these people are not cruel. They simply do not know how to honor emotions.

We could feel reluctant ourselves to share honest emotions with others as we move through our grief. C. S. Lewis observed that he was "an embarrassment" to others as he grieved.[1] It is just as likely that he, not so much others, felt embarrassed. If we find ourselves feeling as Lewis did, we don't need to feel bad about ourselves. We are dealing with a flow of emotions that can be confusing and even disorienting.

As we are able to express emotions, however, we may find others who share or have shared similar feelings. We all live in communities—our families, our friends, our neighborhoods, and our work or study life. Some of them will be able to acknowledge what we feel, not rush to assure us that things will get better, and still allow us to express and experience our emotions.

As we are dealing with our own emotions, other people can be a mirror for us, but they are not merely mirrors. They are humans who live life, feel emotions, and are grateful for someone who appreciates their moods just as we value others who acknowledge ours.

We look for others with whom we can be emotionally honest. Family members are some of the people who know us best. They may be the first with whom we can share our feelings, although family members who are grieving the same loss we are facing may have difficulty supporting us because they are attending to their own grief. A few friends also will be available. Sometimes support groups provide opportunities.

What we will find as we move through our own grief and as we are able to share with others what we are feeling is that we are becoming more sensitive to others. We will be more open to hearing the emotional expressions of others. We may even find ourselves being sought out by those who wish to share their own experiences and emotions. We may become, as Henri Nouwen described, a "wounded healer."[2]

As the poet Chana Bloch wrote in her poem "The Potato Eaters,"

> What does a full stomach know
> of an empty stomach?[3]

Emotional openness with ourselves helps us to be more emotionally open and available to other people.

To Think About

As you look back on your life, think about a time someone was emotionally open about themselves with you. How did that make you feel? Pleased they trusted you? A bit frightened by the emotion? Something else?

To Talk About

Talk with others about what friends or counselors or clergypersons they have found valuable when they are sharing emotions.

To Do

Write a letter to someone who has helped you in the past to let them know what their kindness meant and means to you.

Prayer

God, you are busy creating me. You have given me the ability to feel all kinds of emotions. Some of those I greet happily and some of them I want to stay far away from. Help me to feel at home with myself, among my many thoughts and emotions. In Christ, amen.

My God, my God, why have you forsaken me?
—Psalm 22:1

STAGE

We Feel Depressed and Very Lonely

STAGE

We Feel Depressed and Very Lonely

STAGE THREE

We Feel Depressed and Very Lonely

EVENTUALLY THERE COMES a feeling of utter depression and isolation. It is as if God is no longer in heaven, as if God does not care. It is during these days we are sure that no one else has ever grieved as we are grieving.

It is true; no one has ever grieved exactly as we are grieving because no two people face even the same kind of loss in the same way. But the awful experience of being utterly depressed and isolated is a universal phenomenon. When we find ourselves in the depths of despair, as some readers may be even at this moment, we should remind ourselves that this is to be expected following any significant loss and that such depression is normal and a part of good healthy grief.

The awful experience of being utterly depressed and isolated is a universal phenomenon.

One way to describe a depression is to say it is much like a very dark day when the clouds have so blacked out the sun that everyone says, "The sun isn't shining today." We know that the sun is shining, but it appears as if it is not. Perhaps you have had occasion to take a plane trip on a day like that. Your plane climbs up and up through layers of heavy dark clouds, and you cannot see a thing through the windows. It is as dark as night. Then suddenly your plane breaks through the highest bank of inky black clouds at twenty-eight thousand or perhaps thirty-eight thousand feet, and immediately the sun pours through the window. Everyone looks out upon the white billowy clouds still so black on the other side, and some people exclaim, "Isn't it beautiful!" Then someone says, "Too bad the people downstairs can't see this." But the people downstairs are saying, "The sun isn't shining today." The sun is shining, but something has come between the people and the sun.

This is what a depression is like. Something seems to come between the person and his fellow men so that he feels a tremendous loneliness, an awful sense of isolation. And he can't seem to break through it.

When we are depressed, we find ourselves thinking thoughts we never have otherwise. We say God does not care. We may even doubt that there is a God.

Depression is not something unique just to you or me. It is an experience that seems to come to all people when something or someone they love and treasure dearly is taken away from them. In the Scriptures we hear strong men like David in the Psalms crying out in their isolation, "Why are you cast down, O my soul? . . . My soul is cast down within me, . . . I say to God, my rock, why has Thou forgotten me? . . . My adversaries taunt me, while they say continually, 'Where is your God?'"

And, during the times we are depressed, it is as if, deep inside, we are saying, "Where is my God?" Jesus himself faced this loneliness when on the cross he cried out, "My God, my God, why has thou forsaken me?"

What we must never forget about a depression experience is that one day it will pass. Dark days do not last forever. The clouds are always moving, though very slowly. The person in the midst of a depression is certain, of course, that the clouds are not moving. He is convinced that this is a state in which he will remain the rest of his life. Any attempt to try to convince him otherwise is useless. However, the experience of people through the centuries has been that the dark clouds of depression are moving; they do pass.

The clouds are always moving, though very slowly.

One of the most helpful things we can do for a friend at such a time is to stand by that friend in quiet confidence and assure him or her that this, too, shall pass. The friend will not believe us at first and will tell us we do not know what we are talking about. We may even be asked to leave. But the friend usually does not mean it. Once it is realized that our concern is genuine, then the quiet assertion of our own confidence in God's continuing care and concern will assist tremendously in the friend's recovery.

For some people the clouds roll away seemingly all at once. Something happens within them, or some important event triggers a movement toward the next stage of grief. For others it takes longer, stretching the weeks into months. Such people can be immeasurably helped by the constant, consistent concern of those who really care about them.

A congregation of religious people ought to live up to the well-known description of "the community of the concerned." If they are actually concerned about those who mourn, who feel lost from the world and from God, then they will earn the lasting gratitude of those who mourn.

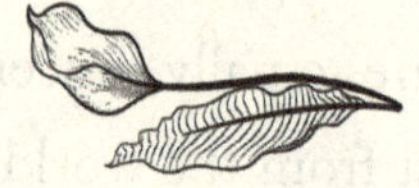

Knowing God's love is steadfast, what are the words you want to say to God right now? How might you identify and reach out to those who acknowledge your deep pain and are ready to stand with you in your sorrow? What are you doing to stay connected to the significant people in your life?

DEVOTIONAL

Take My Hand, Precious Lord

Sometimes we may think that we should go to God the way we go to visit a friend, that is, to make sure we are cleaned up and looking good. But when we find ourselves tired, weak, and worn—the way Dorsey felt when he wrote this song, after his wife and newborn son died—that is when we most need to come to God, just as we are.

In such times we can find ourselves also praying, "Precious Lord . . ." Sometimes that phrase will be an expression of exhaustion as we wonder whether God is present. Sometimes those words will be a plea that God keep God's promises to be with us in times of deep pain.

Does that presence ease the pain and stop the depression and loneliness? Sometimes it does, but there are times when we feel that it doesn't. Well-meaning friends might advise us simply to "turn it over to God" and assure us that things will get better. Still, we might find that "turning over" can be hard to do. And when we are able to move toward God, we don't always feel an improved relationship. We remember that depression puts up an invisible blanket, as C. S. Lewis described it, as something that "comes between." It is there between us and our own self-understanding, our relationships with others, our encounter with creation, and our relationship to God.

It is also important to remember that this blanket, as real as it is, does not block out God. It may feel like that to us at moments of despair, but we are not separated from God. We feel lonely, abandoned, a bit like Jesus in Gethsemane. But we can choose that this sense is not a lasting one. We remember or learn how to pray, we remember or learn how to lament, and we remember and learn how to hope.

We pray to be in conversation with the God who loves us.

We lament because—like Dorsey, like biblical authors, and like Jesus—we know the pain of grief and depression and loneliness.

We hope because the promise we hear—from the Bible, from hymns, from our sisters and brothers—is that God forsakes nothing of what God has made.

The prophet Isaiah, writing to people who thought God had forgotten them, wrote these words:

But Zion said, "The Lord has forsaken me,
    my Lord has forgotten me."
Can a woman forget her nursing child,
    or show no compassion for the child of her womb?
Even these may forget,
    yet I will not forget you.
See, I have inscribed you on the palms of my hands.
—Isaiah 49:14–16

The feelings of depression and loneliness we have after experiencing a loss are real and normal. The God who is with us at those times is real and close as well.

To Think About

Read the words of the hymn that begins this devotion. What thoughts and feelings do you have when you read these words?

To Talk About

With a friend or clergyperson, talk about when and why you sometimes have a hard time believing God is with you in sad times. Talk also about how you experience God in those times.

To Do

Write your own prayer to God about your feelings and what you want from God.

Prayer

Precious Lord, you are always with me. I ask you to help me know that, especially in those times of pain and grief and depression and loneliness, I am not alone but that you have promised to be with me forever. Take my hand, Precious Lord. Amen.

I am poured out like water,
and all my bones are out of joint;
my heart is like wax;
it is melted within my breast;
my mouth is dried up like a potsherd,
and my tongue sticks to my jaws;
you lay me in the dust of death.
—Psalm 22:14–15

STAGE

We May Experience Physical Symptoms of Distress

STAGE FOUR

We May Experience Physical Symptoms of Distress

AS A CLERGYMAN in a medical center, where I have worked closely with doctors and their patients for many years, I have slowly become aware of the fact that many of the patients I see are ill because of some unresolved grief situation. Usually the patient first went to see the doctor with a physical complaint. In an increasing number of cases, these people tell me about some great loss they have sustained during the past months or year or two. As we talk, it is clear they have not yet worked through some of the central problems related to that loss. I see this so often that I cannot help drawing the conclusion that there is a stronger relationship than we have ever thought between illness and the way in which a person handles a great loss.

Many of the patients I see are ill because of some unresolved grief situation.

Some of these people who have physical symptoms of distress have stopped at one of the stages in the ten-stage grief process. Unless someone can help them to work through the emotional problems involved in the stage in which they seem to be fixed, they will remain ill. No amount of medicine will significantly change the situation.

Let me illustrate this psychosomatic problem by giving an example of the type of person I am talking about.

Here is a young couple in their early thirties, Mr. and Mrs. Brown, who live in a small town in Iowa. It could be Illinois or Indiana or any other state. They live in a modest little home, and he works at a job he likes very much. His salary is small, but other things make up for it. He comes home for lunch every noon, and his wife and he have time to putter in the garden together. Every day at five he is home, and they have all their evenings together. Life is rich for them in this community where both of them were born and raised. They have their families here. They happen not to have any children, but their nieces and nephews are in and out of the house all the time, and so they lack for nothing.

Then one day Mr. Brown is asked to take his boss's place on a business trip to a convention in Chicago. There he meets a man who sees such potential in Mr. Brown that he invites him to join his firm, offering him a salary almost three times what he is making in Iowa. Mr. Brown accepts the job, of course! In America, if you get an offer of more money, you take it!

Everyone back home in Iowa is proud of the Browns because they have made good. They are showered with parties and gifts as everyone wishes them well.

Mr. and Mrs. Brown move to a beautiful apartment in Chicago, and everything is just as it is supposed to be in the storybooks, except that Mr. Brown does not come home for lunch any more, and his wife misses him very much. Things go along quite well at first until they find that he frequently has to stay downtown to entertain customers at dinner. Mrs. Brown is not at all happy about this. But the real blow comes when they learn he is to be on the road two or three days a week. This means he does not see his wife from Tuesday until Friday.

What does this do to Mrs. Brown? It changes the whole pattern of her life. Days formerly filled with activity related to her husband, her parents and brothers and sisters, and small-town events are now filled with emptiness and boredom. All she has to do all day is face the four walls of this handsomely decorated apartment. By nature she is not an outgoing person, and she has never had to make her own friends, for they were already there. Her apartment takes on the appearance of a prison as far as she is concerned. She cannot help but resent her husband's new job, for it has taken him away from her. She even begins to resent her husband because when he comes home at night, all he talks about is business and how much money he is making.

Frankly, Mrs. Brown does not care a rap about the money or the success of his business. Secretly she wishes the business would fold up so they could go back to Iowa. Of course, she does not dare say this. She has to put up a good front and pretend she is thrilled with her husband's success. Soon, however, this "phoniness" begins to show up, and both of them sense that something dreadful is happening to them.

Mrs. Brown has suffered a great loss. She is a woman in grief. She does not confide in anyone, even by mail, because it would sound so juvenile. After all, she is supposed to be thrilled by their new and better way of living. Yet she finds herself engulfed by loneliness, a sense of depression, and isolation.

Then she develops physical symptoms of distress: headaches and backaches and all kinds of aches. Weeks go by, and she is miserable. Finally, she has to tell her husband about her physical symptoms, and he insists she see a doctor immediately. The doctor gives her some medications, and she feels better for a time. After a few weeks she has a recurrence of these same symptoms, and the doctor suggests she go into the hospital for a complete checkup.

In the hospital they find nothing physically wrong with Mrs. Brown. Still, she is sick, just as sick as a person with something like a broken leg or an ulcer. The doctor talks with a chaplain or a psychiatrist or a social worker and asks him to look in on Mrs. Brown because he suspects this illness might be related to some family problems. At first Mrs. Brown talks to the chaplain only about pleasant matters. Finding him easy to talk to and not in any hurry, she then begins to say a little bit about how she misses Iowa. Gradually she breaks down and finally, with great emotion, tells the chaplain how she hates her husband's business, how she hates everything connected with this move to Chicago. Her hostility, her feelings of guilt, all these things are intertwined with her grief. This is essentially why she is ill.

In situations like this, where grief is so important a factor in the illness, we can see why doctors and ministers and others, such as social workers and nurses, must join forces so that more than just the physical symptoms can be treated. Mrs. Brown must now be helped to understand the cause of these symptoms. But more than that, she must be helped to work through her feelings of loss.

The minister sees the "working through process" as involving a reexamination of a person's faith—in this case, her way of looking at life. It is no small task, and it may take many months of discussion, self-examination, study, and fellowship with the concerned community of believers.

[Working through grief] is no small task, and it may take many months.

In Mrs. Brown's case, it might be that her problem is related to the fact that she did not have the usual growing-up experiences that most people have at the age of eighteen or twenty. Her present difficult experience is a delayed reaction. Now at the age of thirty-two she has to face leaving home and family and losing her husband, all at once.

The easiest solution would seem to be that Mr. Brown quit his job and go back to Iowa and live as they did before. But then Mrs. Brown's guilt would be compounded, for she would feel guilty of keeping her husband from a promising future. And now that he has had a taste of business success, we cannot imagine he would be happy in his former job. No, these people came to the crossroads and made a decision that forever changed their lives.

They cannot turn back and take up where they left off because they are no longer the same two people. They will never really be able to face the new kinds of problems that life presents until they have seriously thought through and reconstructed their basic philosophy of life.

Although Mr. and Mrs. Brown might never think of their problem as being at the core a philosophical and religious one, in essence that is what it is. Every man and every woman, in order to live a rich and meaningful life, must take a turn at being a philosopher, to search for meaning in living. This move to Chicago has forced both Mr. and Mrs. Brown to rethink what they consider to be worth striving for.

The Christian faith offers a stimulating context in which to do this rethinking. It is the desire of every good pastor to encourage people like Mr. and Mrs. Brown to discuss in depth such life-shaping beliefs, in order that their faith may develop a maturity commensurate with their chronological age.

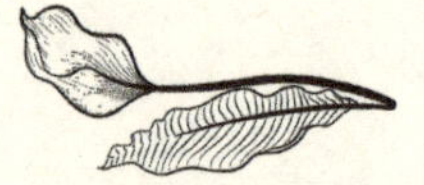

How might you lessen the expectations you have for your behavior as you move through the grief process? How are you able to identify your physical symptoms of grief? Do you need to seek help, or can you address them on your own?

DEVOTIONAL

The Distress of Grief

Granger Westberg noticed in his time with people experiencing grief that physical symptoms of distress are common because the mind and the body are never separate. God's love and God's promise are given to us as whole people whose bodies, minds, emotions, experiences, and histories all receive God's grace.

This simply means that when our minds are troubled, it isn't unusual for our bodies to feel signs of trouble as well. We all have experienced upset stomachs when we're anticipating something special or significant—a test in school, a new job, a new home, a marriage. All these, even good things, can stress us and influence our feelings.

What the author writes about in this stage of grief is the physical symptoms that may follow a stressful event. Stress and distress can be de-stressed by conversations with friends and helpers and, as the psalmist shows, conversations with God.

The author shares an account of the Browns, who move from a small town in Iowa to Chicago for the sake of the husband's promotion. The wife begins to experience physical distress. With the help of a chaplain, she is able to recognize the cause of the illness is her anger, guilt, and grief at the move. Reexamining her life helps her to move into healing.

Grief comes to us in many ways and at many ages. With that grief comes distress and the disruption of our lives.

A student's roommate breaks up with her boyfriend. The student wants to remain friends with her roommate's former boyfriend but feels that would betray her roommate. She is angry at both of them for her dilemma. As a result, she loses sleep and her school work suffers. Her campus pastor explores the situation with her and suggests reframing the situation (give her friends the benefit of the doubt) and talking with them both about her desire to maintain friendships with both of them. The student bears love and forgiveness for herself and for her friends and moves on into the semester with her two friends and renewed strength.

The Christian name for this process of reframing is *repentance*. That doesn't mean only being sorry for sin but reflects the Hebrew word that means to "turn around" (*shuv*) and the Greek word that means "to have one's mind changed" (*metanoia*).

For Mrs. Brown in *Good Grief*, the physical distress she experienced was certainly not a good thing. None of us enjoy feeling ill! But it became for her, and it can become for us, an inspiration and a reason for looking at our lives, turning around, and having our minds changed as we prepare to move into the future.

To Think About

When has the stress of an event or grief caused you physical distress? When you feel such distress, where in your body does it occur? In your head, your chest, your stomach, your muscles? Try to remember how you were able to feel better when your body has reacted to stress.

To Talk About

Talk with a friend about the experiences each of you may have had following stressful events or times of grief. Have they caused you to rethink aspects of your life? Discuss the changes that rethinking brought about.

To Do

Make a list of those things in your life that you have considered most important to you. Include what used to be important but is no longer as well as things you now find important that you didn't earlier.

Prayer

Gracious God, I thank you that you are always willing to listen to me, always willing to hold me, always willing to comfort me. When I am ill or distressed, help me to keep that good news in my heart. In Jesus's name, amen.

God is our refuge and strength,
a very present help in trouble.
Therefore, we will not fear, though the earth should change,
though the mountains shake in the heart of the sea;
though its waters roar and foam,
though the mountains tremble with its tumult.
—Psalm 46:1–3

STAGE

We May Become Panicky

STAGE FIVE

We May Become Panicky

WE FIND OURSELVES becoming panicky because we can think of nothing but the loss. We try so hard to get our minds off the subject, and perhaps for a moment or two we can be distracted, but soon we are right back again where we started. Naturally, this hinders our effectiveness in anything we are trying to do. We find that we are not producing the work of which we are capable. We start worrying about our mental health. When people ask us questions, we have to ask them to repeat so often that they wonder what is wrong with us. We simply cannot concentrate.

Inability to concentrate in time of grief is just as natural as it can be.

All sorts of unpleasant thoughts come to us, as we recall people we have known who have had to go to mental hospitals after they have experienced some great loss.

Inability to concentrate in time of grief is just as natural as it can be. It would be stranger still if we could easily put aside our grief for routine matters. When something has been terribly important to us for a long time and it is taken from us, we cannot help but be constantly drawn to the lost object. And we suffer daily as we struggle with the gradually dawning realization that it is gone forever.

When a person begins worrying about losing his mind, he often panics. He becomes almost paralyzed with fear. It is often fear of the unknown, or fear of something he does not understand, that throws him into this panic.

It is important that we understand something about the grief process in advance of the crisis so that we may eliminate the panic that accompanies fear of the unknown. When we have been briefed about some of the tricks that grief plays on our minds, then we are not overwhelmed by the disturbing thoughts that seek to take over. It is the panic of thinking we are going through something wholly abnormal that throws us deeper into despair. But it is not abnormal; it is normal! It is comforting to know that even panic is normal.

Grief plays tricks on our minds.

To help ourselves through such a period when we can think of nothing but our loss, we must be open to new and different human relationships. At a time like this, all we want to do is run away from life. The last thing we care to do is to try anything new. We can think of a hundred different reasons why we prefer to stay home and be gloomy rather than go out and be forced to be nice to people and think new thoughts. Such an attitude is natural; it is to be expected. We must not, however, wallow in our gloom, for it will only prolong our grief work. And to work through grief is very hard work!

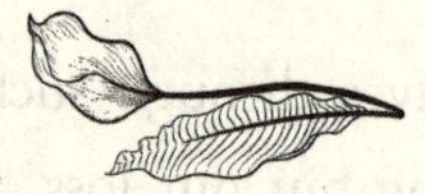

What situations have arisen that cause you panic? What could you do to ground yourself at those times?

DEVOTIONAL

Am I Losing My Mind?

> *Inability to concentrate in time of grief is just as natural as it can be. It would be stranger still if we could easily put aside our grief for routine matters. When something has been terribly important to us for a long time and it is taken from us, we cannot help but be constantly drawn to the lost object. And we suffer daily as we struggle with the gradually dawning realization that it is gone forever.*
>
> —Granger E. Westberg

We cannot escape our daily obligations of rising, eating, dressing, cleaning, working or studying, running errands, checking things off our to-do lists, and so on. They are hard to escape, and they are not always pleasant to pursue. When grief is weighing on us and the realization of loss is an ongoing presence in our lives, the daily tasks can become daily grinds.

The distraction of grief, especially if we have always been consistent and careful about our daily tasks, can worry us. Granger Westberg writes that this stage is one of "panic" in that we worry our lack of attention might mean greater problems with our emotional and mental health.

Popular music has plenty of examples of singers worrying about losing their minds, either because something amazing has happened or, more often, because of a lost love. Yes, "losing my mind" may be just a figure of speech, but for people deeply experiencing this stage of grief, the worry, the panic, is real. We may wonder, "What if this is how I'm going to be the rest of my life? Am I losing my mind?"

While we may not choose the word *panic* to describe how we feel—rather, anxious, worried, obsessed—that word portrays an inner scene of turmoil and apprehension about the future.

Those Pedestrian Birds

Those pedestrian birds
whose duty it is to greet the sun,
wake the sleeping: robins, cardinals, a sparrow or two.

Daily tasks performed
from habit, not desire,

The tune whistled in the garden,
morning coffee,
regular routines of jog or dog walk.

the walls of the room,
Life itself.

These you note and make notes
to love and honor.

Still, the sun rises,
the heat of the day flattens
your narrow appreciations.

You move, almost intentionally,
toward evening.

We can often see ourselves moving almost intentionally through the day toward evening, not really aware of ourselves or our tasks. We feel that we are simply doing the motions. The author's suggestion is that a healthy thing for us to do in this stage when we feel panic is to "be open to new and different human relationships."

To Think About

When has simply living out daily tasks and responsibilities been hard for you? What was going on at these times? What did you find helpful, and what did you find unhelpful? Why do you find some things helpful? Why do you find some things unhelpful?

To Talk About

Talk with a friend about times when you worried about the future. What were your situations then? How did you feel, and how did you move beyond that worry?

To Do

Write down five events you would like to see happen in the future, whether in days, weeks, months, years, or multiple timeframes. After some thought, write down one step next to each event that you can take to help make it happen.

Prayer

God, my source of strength and hope, be with me when my own grief and worry weigh me down and the future seems more threat than promise. Bless me with your Spirit and open me to the days ahead. In Jesus's name, amen.

When the righteous cry for help, the Lord hears,
and rescues them from all their troubles.
The Lord is near to the brokenhearted
and saves the crushed in spirit.
—Psalm 34:17–18

STAGE

We Feel a Sense of Guilt about the Loss

STAGE SIX

We Feel a Sense of Guilt about the Loss

AT THE VERY outset, we should make the distinction between "normal" guilt and neurotic guilt. Generally speaking, normal guilt is the guilt we feel when we have done something, or neglected to do something, for which we ought, by the standards of our society, to feel guilty. Neurotic guilt is feeling guilty all out of proportion to our own real involvement in a particular problem.

Let me illustrate real guilt or normal guilt. When we lose a loved one through death, it would be hard to conceive of any of us who had lived closely with the departed one who would not feel guilty about some of the things we did not do for this person when he or she was alive, or the things we did do that hurt this person. We know we have sinned against this person by thought, word, and deed, and our religious training says we should face up to our sin, and we ought to feel guilty about it.

For the mature religious person, guilt is not something new. In handling this sixth stage of grief, such a person has some advantage over one who has never heard much about sin and grace. He or she has experienced the remarkable sense of release that comes when we admit guilt in the prayer of confession. Such persons know about the divine gift of forgiveness and acceptance, so they do not fear admission of guilt. They know that real guilt must never be glossed over, nor should it be repressed. They have learned to come to terms with it. And these terms include a sense of being alienated from God, genuine repentance, followed by honest confession.

Contrite confession of real guilt is a part of every worship service. We all have need to say, "Have mercy upon me, O God. Create in me a clean heart, O God, and renew a right spirit within me."

Have mercy upon me, O God.

There is also such a thing as neurotic guilt, and it is often intertwined with real guilt. It is difficult ever to separate one from the other completely. Every person has some neurotic-guilt feelings. It is a matter of degree. Everyone ought to be aware of these neurotic tendencies and not be lulled into thinking that it is only the other person who uses such mental mechanisms to escape reality.

An illustration of neurotic guilt might be a daughter who has stayed by her aged mother's bedside in the hospital for days and days without sleep. The doctor now orders her to go home and get some sleep. This turns out to be the night that her mother dies, and she will never forgive herself for not being there when it happened. She broods endlessly about this and builds it up out of proportion to the real situation.

If only she could talk over the problem with somebody who understands that this guilt is but a symptom of something deeper, she would begin to understand how to cope with her neurotic guilt and not have to be so unhappy. If she does not work through these problems at this time, they may hinder her full movement back into life again.

It is important for us to face both our normal guilt and our neurotic guilt.

Unresolved guilt and misunderstood emotions of this type can make us miserable for years, or they might come out in a variety of physical symptoms of distress. It is important for us to face both our normal guilt and our neurotic guilt. We must not be afraid or embarrassed to talk about our feelings of guilt with those who have been trained to help us.

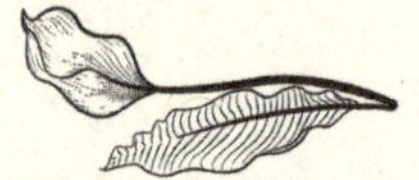

Which of your "if onlys" could help you determine whether you need consolation or forgiveness? Who are the people who might help you? How can Psalm 51 help you work through both false and genuine guilt? The psalmist experienced both types of guilt. What psalms are helpful to you now?

DEVOTIONAL

We Can't Avoid It

Now Peter was sitting outside in the courtyard. A servant-girl came to him and said, "You also were with Jesus the Galilean." But he denied it before all of them, saying, "I do not know what you are talking about." When he went out to the porch, another servant-girl saw him, and she said to the bystanders, "This man was with Jesus of Nazareth." Again he denied it with an oath, "I do not know the man." After a little while the bystanders came up and said to Peter, "Certainly you are also one of them, for your accent betrays you." Then he began to curse, and he swore an oath, "I do not know the man!" At that moment the cock crowed. Then Peter remembered what Jesus had said: "Before the cock crows, you will deny me three times." And he went out and wept bitterly.

—Matthew 26:69–75

What do we do with guilt?

Because we are human, we can't avoid guilt. We all not only make mistakes but do things that hurt other people. Peter had been a loyal follower of Jesus. But when Jesus was arrested and led away, Peter looked after his own safety. He denied even knowing Jesus. The cock crowed and Peter, feeling his guilt, wept bitterly.

What do we do with guilt?

Our response may depend on what kind of guilt we feel, but often we react the same way for both "normal" and "neurotic" guilt.

We might deny we feel any guilt, look for an excuse, or downplay damage we might have done. We might push it down inside us as far as we can. We might blame the other person for putting us in a position where we "had to do" what we did.

When we are dealing with the guilt that is part of the grief process, chances are the person we blame is ourselves. "Why didn't I call an ambulance?!" "How come I didn't learn CPR when I had a chance?" "I should have told him not to drive in the snow!" "Why did I ask her to stop by with all the construction going on?"

"Why didn't I visit last summer?" "I sure wish I hadn't told him the story he wrote was stupid." Sometimes the way we deal with guilt is to hate ourselves. This may be the least helpful option—except for refusing to deal with it at all.

We might be feeling regret for something we did or didn't do or say. Such regret is natural, but we experience it as guilt, sorrow for something we did or didn't do that we wish we could change but can't. And that sense of powerlessness is frustrating for us.

Then again, if we are feeling neurotic guilt, guilt that is unrealistic and not based on something wrong or harmful we've done, it can be harder for us to face it. We can let it eat at us (as we can with all guilt) and hope it goes away by itself, or we can just pretend that this is simply the way it is for humans.

Of Course There's Always Guilt

Waiting in the dark
under the last stair,
gray scales, narrow eyes
breath hissing

through yellow teeth,
waiting
there.

The sooner we can deal with our guilt, the healthier we'll be. If we feel guilt for something that is our own fault, the result of our own action or inaction, the best thing for us is to go to the person we believe we hurt. We confess, we apologize, we ask forgiveness. We hope the apology is accepted, but at least we have expressed the guilt and put it "out there." If guilt involves a person whose death we are mourning, it might be healing for us to talk to a friend or family member to express our remorse. A trusted counselor can also help us as we deal with our guilt and move on into our relationships.

To Think About

We all have felt guilt. Think about times in your life when you felt guilty about something you did or said. Focus on just a few times and try to remember both how you felt and how you dealt with it.

To Talk About

Talk with a friend about their own experience of guilt. This doesn't have to be a serious and somber conversation; feel free to express the humor in the situation. But talk together about how you each take care of guilt you have felt.

To Do

If you are feeling guilty about something you said or did that hurt someone, talk to that person, apologize, and ask their forgiveness.

Prayer

Dear gracious and loving God, you are more ready to forgive than we are to acknowledge or confess our sin or guilt. You do indeed forgive. Help me not to be ashamed of guilt but to admit it. Help me not to dwell on guilt but to move on to forgiveness. Help me to forgive myself. Help me to forgive others as well. In Christ, amen.

For he will command his angels concerning you
to guard you in all your ways.
On their hands they will bear you up,
so that you will not dash your foot against a stone.
—Psalm 91:11–12

STAGE

We Are Filled with Anger and Resentment

STAGE SEVEN

We Are Filled with Anger and Resentment

GRADUALLY WE MOVE up out of the depression, and in so doing may be more able to express some of the strong feelings of anger and resentment of which we may not even have been aware.

When we say anger and resentment are a part of "good grief," we probably should qualify this to some extent. We do not wish to leave the impression that persons in grief ought to be encouraged to be angry or resentful. What we are saying is that these feelings are normal for every human and that even the most devout persons can very well feel angry and resentful, even though we try very hard to sublimate these feelings. It would be most harmful to us if we could not admit to ourselves, to God, and to our friends that we, being human, need to confess our anger and resentfulness and ask for strength to rise above it.

Another way to put it is to say that resentment is not a healthy emotion and, if allowed to take over, it can be very, very harmful. Yet it is a normal part of the grief process. It is to be expected, it is to be wrestled with, and it can, by the grace of God, be overcome.

When we have something precious taken from us, we inevitably go through a stage when we are very critical of everything and everyone who was related to the loss. We spare no one in our systematic scrutiny of the event, attempting to understand exactly why this thing happened and who is to blame. The human is always looking for someone to blame. If we have lost someone through death, we express hostility toward anyone who cared for the patient. We are hostile to the doctor because he operated, or we are hostile to him because he did not operate. No matter what he did, it was wrong. While we are in this mood, we look at everyone with a jaundiced eye.

Even the most devout persons can very well feel angry and resentful.

If we talk to the minister and are encouraged to admit what we really think, one day we may say, "Why did God do this to me?" or "How can he be a God of love if he treats people like this?" With Thomas Carlyle we cynically say, "God sits in his heaven and does nothing."

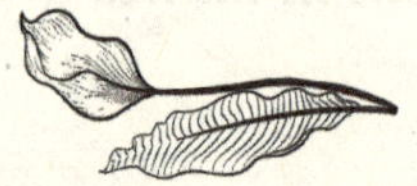

Watching life go on for others may produce strong feelings, including anger and resentment. In what safe ways have you expressed those emotions in other situations? Expressing anger and resentment can be a helpful part of the healing process. How might journaling or sharing your feelings help you to grieve?

DEVOTIONAL

Letting Go of Anger and Resentment

> *So when you are offering your gift at the altar, if you remember that your brother or sister has something against you, leave your gift there before the altar and go; first be reconciled to your brother or sister, and then come and offer your gift.*
>
> —Matthew 5:23–24

Anger and resentment in our grief process primarily affect us. But we might focus not on ourselves but on other events and people. When we do that, our relationships are negatively affected. Once significant relationships with friends, family members, or coworkers become strained. We may resent those who are happier than we are. Our anger may keep us from seeking out others for conversation.

Holding on to anger and resentment is like making a tight fist. While that fist is tight, we cannot reach out to another, we cannot give anything to or receive anything from another. Eventually, the stress on our muscles—in our hands, up our arms, even into our shoulders, back, and neck—makes us uncomfortable and less willing to interact with others.

Anger and resentment can also have a spillover effect. When we are under the influence of these feelings and focusing on specific people or events, we will tend to distort our relationships. We might see others as if in an amusement park mirror—distorted and unreal. We might easily find things to complain about, whether specific people, ordinary experiences in our own daily lives, or world events.

If you have had this experience, you know that this is not a particularly enjoyable way to live. We can isolate ourselves, ignore friendships, fail to seek advice and counsel.

We may be angry at other people for a valid reason. Someone may have caused an accident. Someone may have supplied drugs or alcohol that lead to a death. Someone may have tried to help and made things worse. Someone may have refused to help, and the grief deepened.

We may have reason to resent others. Some may seem not to share our grief, even though they may be as involved in the loss as we are. Some may have said hurtful things to us, perhaps minimizing our grief or criticizing the person or thing we have lost. Some may have begun a return to normal life and happiness before we did and before we think they should.

Feeling such resentment toward other people can be difficult for us, but the most healing activity we can do is to take steps to restore these relationships. We should first determine whether our anger and resentment are based on actual events. We do that by considering why we are angry or resentful. A trusted friend, counselor, or clergyperson will be a valuable coworker with us in moving through this phase to healing and hope. They can listen to us, help us hear ourselves more accurately, and propose alternatives to anger and resentment.

If we do need to talk with the person from whom we feel estranged, we take a deep breath and contact the person. Sometimes the physical act of a deep breath alone will prepare us. It will also be good to pray for an open spirit as we begin the conversation. If we have a complaint, we try to state it in a way that isn't accusing but focuses on our own feelings. We don't say "you make me angry" but "I'm feeling angry about something you said [or did]." Conversation can clear up your feelings about it and your relationship with that person. It takes work. But holding on to anger and resentment also takes work.

As we deal with the feelings and choose to move forward, we can say:

Someone may have wronged me.

I choose not to wrong myself.

I will forgive them.

To Think About

Consider what things are worth your anger. What things have you been angry about that were not worth your anger? Think about your criteria and reasons for the distinction.

To Talk About

Do you know someone you consider to be particularly good at letting go of anger or grudges and who seems not to become resentful? If so, sit down with them, relate your sense of how they treat anger and resentment, and ask for their advice in dealing with the feelings.

To Do

Has someone hurt or angered you? Think about what you would like to say to this person. Meet with that person after first adopting a willingness to forgive.

Prayer

Gracious God, thank you for placing me in a larger community of people. I really love many of them. Thank you for them. Some of them get me angry. And I'm angry at some for no good reason. Give me your Spirit. Clear my heart and mind and help me seek reconciliation and a restored relationship with my brothers and sisters. In Jesus's name, amen.

When you pass through the waters, I will be with you;
and through the rivers, they shall not overwhelm you;
when you walk through fire you shall not be burned,
and the flame shall not consume you

—Isaiah 43:2

STAGE

We Resist Returning

STAGE EIGHT

We Resist Returning

ALTHOUGH WE MAY be quite well along in our grief work and really want to get back to our usual activities, something inside us resists returning. Our loss has been something special, and we feel that other people just do not understand how great the loss was. They are off talking about other things, and we are left alone with our sorrow. Everyone has forgotten our tragedy. Somebody has to keep the memory of it alive. We must not allow things to get back to normal again.

The pace of modern life may have something to do with this. The minute people finish one event they are off to another and another. And if they do not have enough happening in their lives, they live out other exciting events vicariously through television. Most people do not take time to help work through one another's losses. We seldom feel we have accomplished the work of grieving.

We also find that when we attempt to get back into life again, it is much too painful. We would rather grieve than fight the battle of coping with new situations. Grieving is painful, but not as painful as having to face entirely new decisions every hour. We are more comfortable in our grief than in the new unpredictable world. We want to stay with the familiar.

We are more comfortable in our grief than in the new unpredictable world.

There are other related reasons for resisting the return. Our modern way of life makes it so difficult for us to grieve about any loss in the presence of other people. We are forced to carry all the grief within ourselves.

This is particularly true in the loss of a loved one through death. When many of us were children, people grieved more openly. The men wore black armbands, and the women wore black veils for six months to a year while in mourning for a loved one so that everyone was reminded daily of their loss. One of the last public personages to wear a black armband was President Franklin Roosevelt at the death of his mother.

In some parts of Europe, people continue to wear symbols of grieving. But we somehow have the impression that grief is out of place in our society. We conduct a quiet conspiracy of silence against it. We try never to talk about grief and certainly never display it by any outward sign. We offer our sympathy to our grieving friends immediately after their loss has occurred, but from then on we say in effect, "Now, let's get back to business as usual."

A typical illustration is the experience of a widow, whose husband died a year or so before, who is with a group of friends who knew her husband. As they are talking together, one of them recalls a very humorous story about her husband. He is about to tell it, and then he thinks to himself, "Oh no, I must not reopen the wound. I must be considerate of her." Consequently he carefully steers away from any conversation about her husband, as does everyone else.

We have the impression that grief is out of place in our society.

Actually, if he had told this story, she doubtless would have laughed heartily and been most pleased. He might have seen a tear or two in her eyes. If he had said, "I'm sorry. I should not have told that story," her response in all probability would have been, "Don't say that! You are the first person in weeks who has even mentioned my husband. No one ever talks about him anymore. It is a wonderful feeling to know that someone still remembers him."

This is part of the task of friends—to help keep the memory of loved ones alive, to show concern for one another, particularly when someone has suffered a great loss. Most people who are grieving are very considerate of others. They do not wish to force their troubles on other people. The quality of our personal interest in these people can demonstrate that we do want to share their burdens with them.

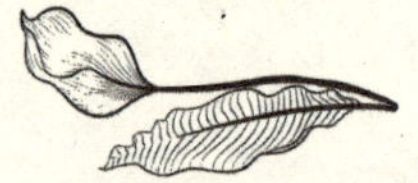

How can you seek out family members and friends who are not only still listening to you but sharing their own memories as well? How do you respond when others assume you are "over" the loss? What might you do to help them help you?

DEVOTIONAL

For the Winter Is Now Past

Coming through a journey of loss and grief is much like approaching the end of a winter. Whether that winter is one of blowing winds and blizzards or cool rains, when it ends most of us see the world coming back to life and life taking on a brighter color. But sometimes the effects of winter continue into spring. We need to make repairs following storms, pick up fallen branches, rake leaves and cut back perennials, replace storm windows with screens, or clean up messes the snow had hidden.

We might experience the closing of our grief journey in a similar way. We will likely encounter holdovers from the colder times. Those old snowdrifts can have an impact on our willingness to engage with the world, with creation.

Most likely, the places and things that helped us appreciate creation will not be the same for us. Certain meals, certain drinks, certain songs, certain places remind us of the pain we experienced. Something we loved, perhaps with another person, may bring reminders of our loss. A place we used to visit may be saying, "The loved one who came here with you will not come here again." That can be hard. We may wonder if we want to revisit these memories.

We will have changed through our grief. For most of us, how we think, how we feel, and how we perceive will be different. But when we let ourselves wonder whether what pleased us before our loss will continue to please or whether we will continue to enjoy what sustained us in our loss, we may be engaging in a second-guessing that will keep us from acting at all.

The only way we can figure out what will continue to give us joy is to try those things out again. We visit those places, listen to that music, share those meals, look and listen and pay attention to the world outside and our own internal reactions.

The lovers in the Song of Songs experience each other and the world with a sense of awe about the wonder of their relationship and the world around them. Bird song, scent of flowers, and fragrance of vine and fig add to the appreciation each one has of the self and the other. Creation is their partner—and ours—in relishing the fullness of God's grace and God's presence with each person.

Reluctance to return to a more active life in the world around us is understandable when we have felt the pain of loss in the same world. But a return will also open the way to new meaning and meaningful encounters with the world around us.

To Think About

In your loss and grief, what places in your world do you not want to revisit? What about these places no longer pleases you? To what places would you like to return? What are the sounds, tastes, or scents you still enjoy?

To Talk About

Have a conversation with a friend about the things you like most in the world around you. If your friend talks about something you have not experienced but that attracts you, ask how to encounter that yourself.

To Do

Is there a place you used to love to go but have not visited for some time, perhaps because of a loss you have experienced? Make a specific plan to revisit that place.

Prayer

Dear God, open your world to me. Help me to see beauty and meaning around me. Help me to explore creation. Help me to find myself in the world around me. In Christ, amen.

Let us hold fast to the confession of our hope without wavering, for he who has promised is faithful.

—Hebrews 10:23

STAGE

Gradually Hope Comes Through

STAGE NINE

Gradually Hope Comes Through

NOW AND THEN we get a little glimpse of hope in one experience or another. This cloud that had been so dark begins to break up, and rays of light come through. We may be in deep grief anywhere from a few weeks to many months. We are never quite sure how long grief is going to last. We must remember that no two people are the same, nor are any two grief situations identical.

We are never quite sure how long grief is going to last.

It would be wrong for us to leave the impression that we are less than human if we do not express our feelings overtly. Some people just do not express emotion and do not need to. Within themselves they probably struggle with many of these stages, but somehow temperamentally they are able to handle these problems very well by themselves. They do not need or want anyone "meddling" in their lives by trying to help them through their grief. We soon learn, if we try to force ourselves upon someone like this, that it is better to let the person work out the problem for himself or herself and call on us if and when we are needed.

The great majority of us, however, need to express our emotions. We need the warm affection and encouragement of those about us. As we are the recipients of such affection, it makes it easier for us to sense that our present attitude of shutting out all new opportunities for meaningful living is unrealistic. We find that other experiences in life can be meaningful again.

We find that other experiences in life can be meaningful again.

The opposite of this is seen in the rich old widow who has acted strangely ever since her musician husband died twenty years ago. She has kept his music studio just as he left it when he died. She had locked the keyboard of his piano and has allowed no one ever to enter the room. Each day she stands for a long time in the doorway with her memories. She has consistently refused to reenter life again. She is known by all as "that eccentric old lady."

Knowing what we do now about the grief process, it appears that at the time of her husband's death she was not helped to wrestle her way through to a new way of life. Apparently she had few or no friends who were willing to stay by her side during those difficult days, and as a result she had no one to encourage her to do her grieving in the normal way. She felt that her only friend was her deceased husband, and she had to remain loyal to him. That was why she locked the keyboard of the piano. She wanted no one else ever to play that piano again, lest she would be disloyal to the memory of the only person whose friendship she could trust.

Rabbi Joshua Liebman's book *Peace of Mind* has an excellent chapter, "Grief's Slow Wisdom," that speaks most effectively to this temptation not to return to usual activities.

Says Liebman: "The melody that the loved one played upon the piano of your life will never be played quite that way again, but we must not close the keyboard and allow the instrument to gather dust. We must seek out other artists of the spirit, new friends who gradually will help us to find the road to life again, who will walk that road with us."

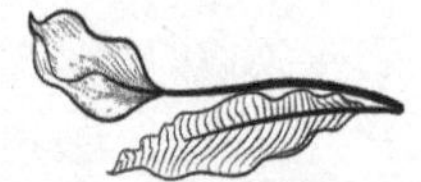

What symbols of the past are you still holding onto? If they are not helpful, how might you let them go?
What steps have you taken to work through your grief? How could you repeat them when fresh grief breaks into your sense of hope?

DEVOTIONAL

Simple Things

When he was at the table with them, he took bread, blessed and broke it, and gave it to them. Then their eyes were opened, and they recognized him; and he vanished from their sight. They said to each other, "Were not our hearts burning within us while he was talking to us on the road, while he was opening the scriptures to us?"

—Luke 24:30–32

Two disciples are walking toward the village of Emmaus. This is Easter Sunday. Jesus appears next to them and asks what they are talking about, and they express surprise he hasn't heard about the prophet from Nazareth. "We had hoped he would be the one to redeem Israel," they say. They had heard rumors of the resurrection but weren't sure what to think or believe. Jesus speaks to them of "the things about himself in all the scriptures," but their eyes aren't open until he breaks bread with them.

They found their hope had been granted, though not in the way they had expected.

God comes to us most often in simple things. When hope begins to return to us in our grief journey, we rarely experience an earth-shattering event that removes all doubt and sorrow and replaces them with pure faith and joy. Rather, we become aware of the presence of the Creator in the ordinary. We meet God in a sunrise or sunset, in the rich variety of the world around us, in the goodness of human love and relationships, and in shared meals with loved ones. That breaking of the bread can whisper something of God's presence.

Even as God moves in and settles with us in the ordinary, we encounter God in the places where God has promised to be present. Worshiping with our faith community, receiving the holy bread and wine, may, without our anticipating it, move us more deeply than it has in the past. A woman attending Easter worship after the death of her husband hears the pastor, speaking of Mary Magdalene, say, "Maybe only those who have experienced grief can see angels," and the grace and mercy of God gently warm her.

As with our other relationships, our relationship with God has changed in the course of our loss and grief. We may give up our assumptions about a God who is all sunshine and happiness, and encounter a God who knows mangers and tombs, life and death—a God who gladly meets us at our best and at our worst and continues to love us.

Sometimes we will feel absolutely certain of God's presence and love. And sometimes we will again wonder if we can count on God. We have experienced that doubt in the past, and it will continue to be part of our faith walk. We don't panic or despair when those times arrive. We know they will not last. We ask ourselves what, if anything, may have brought that on and we claim God's promise that, as we have experienced in the past, the faith that is a nestling faith will again be ours.

In the ordinary and the sacred, hope gradually enters our lives, our daily experiences, and blesses our ordinariness. We hear a word that tells us the future that had seemed closed and distant now is open and promising and comes to us in many ways. We discover that God has not been absent and now returned, but that the God who is abounding in steadfast love has been with us through our grieving and will walk with us into the future.

To Think About

Looking back over your life, when has it been easy to hope in God? When has such hope been more difficult? Ask yourself what might be the reasons for each experience.

To Talk About

"Maybe only those who have experienced grief can see angels." Share that sentence with a friend and discuss what it means and whether you agree with it. What do you each think *angels* might be?

To Do

Read the twenty-fourth chapter of Luke. Then put yourself in the scene as the third disciple on the road. Write down what you would have said in the conversation and what you might have felt at the breaking of the bread.

Prayer

God of hope and life, Jesus, you who love me, you met the disciples on the road to Emmaus and did not end but blessed their journey. You have been with me. You are giving me hope for my future. Continue to walk with me; continue to bless my future, I ask you, amen.

But we do not want you to be uninformed, brothers and sisters, about those who have died, so that you may not grieve as others do who have no hope.

—1 Thessalonians 4:13

STAGE

We Struggle to Affirm Reality

STAGE TEN

We Struggle to Affirm Reality

WE FINALLY BEGIN to affirm reality. Please note that we do not say that the final stage is "We become our old selves again." When we go through any significant grief experience, we come out of it as different people. Depending upon the way we respond to this event, we are either stronger people than we were before or weaker, either healthier in spirit or sicker.

As I have watched hundreds of people go through earthshaking experiences of grief, I have seen that those whose religious faith is mature and healthy come through the experience in a way that makes them better able to help others who face similar tragedies. I have seen people develop a deeper faith in God as a result of their grief experiences.

I have seen people develop a deeper faith in God.

Those who have an immature or childish faith tend to face the loss in a variety of unhealthy ways. Some never really work through their grief and months, even years, later are still fighting battles within themselves. Persons who are spiritually more mature seem to be able to wrestle more effectively because they are aided by the conviction that God is with them. They do not feel that they have to face the present and the future alone.

I am convinced of the importance of keeping at the task of nurturing one's faith because I have seen how such people demonstrate greatness under trial. Conversely, I now have seen what happens to people who have not taken seriously the necessity of working at their faith when the going was good. These people seem unprepared to handle even the smaller losses that face all of us from time to time.

People of faith do not just suddenly get that way. Like the athlete who must stay in training, these people are always in training for whatever may come at any time. When loss comes, they are ready for it. It is just one of many griefs they have learned to wrestle with creatively. They grieve deeply over their loss, to be sure, and they, too, go through the stages of grief we have described, but they eventually come to understand that everything has not been taken from them. They realize that life will never be the same again, but they begin to sense that there is much in life that can be affirmed. And to affirm something is to say that it is good.

At the time of great loss, people who have a mature faith give evidence of an uncommon relationship with God. And they demonstrate an uncommon inner sense of strength and poise that grows out of their confidence that such a relationship with God can never be taken away from them. With such a basic philosophy, they can face any earthly loss with the knowledge that they still have not lost everything. They still have God on whom to rely. I have come to see that this way of looking at life makes an amazing difference in the quality of the grief experience. It actually can become good grief!

It is not right that people should try to carry on grief work alone. People through the centuries have found new and unexpected strength in the words, "I am with you always." So we say, "Grieve—not as those who have no hope," but please, when you have something worth grieving about, go ahead and grieve.

Grieve—not as those who have no hope.

As we begin to struggle to affirm reality, we find that we need not be afraid of the real world. We can live in it again. We can even love it again. For a time we thought there was nothing about life that we could affirm. Now the dark clouds are beginning to break up, and occasionally, for brief moments, rays of the sun come through. And hope, based on faith in a God whom our fathers and mothers have found to be dependable, once more becomes a part of our own outlook on life. Though we continue to struggle, we do affirm reality!

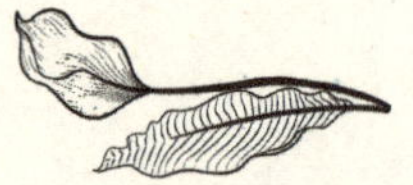

Accepting loss is a slow and gradual process with steps backward as well as forward. What experiences have you had that have taught you something you can use in the future? In what ways could your grief experience help someone else who is dealing with loss?

DEVOTIONAL

Not as Those Who Have No Hope

Now concerning love of the brothers and sisters, you do not need to have anyone write to you, for you yourselves have been taught by God to love one another. . . . But we do not want you to be uninformed, brothers and sisters, about those who have died, so that you may not grieve as others do who have no hope. For since we believe that Jesus died and rose again, even so, through Jesus, God will bring with him those who have died.

—1 Thessalonians 4:9–14

Granger Westberg notes many times in his book, but especially in his summary of stage ten, that a mature and practiced faith is essential for us as we are moving through grief and, of course, moving through our lives.

A mature faith is not based on simply reciting creeds or principles and agreeing with what they say. While statements of faith are important, faith is a relationship with God. Paul writes to the Thessalonians about their love for their brothers and sisters but also their love for outsiders. This, like all of our relationships, is connected to God's love for them and their love for and their faith in God.

Faith, our relationship with God, can be a relationship that wrestles. It contends now and then, it asks questions, it wonders why and how and is not afraid, like the writers of the Bible, to challenge God.

Faith can also be a relationship that nestles. Like a child or a young bird, it finds comfort simply in resting in God, in being comforted and nourished by God. I once was a guest preacher at a church in a small town in Wisconsin. Behind the altar was a gold-tinted window in the shape of a cross. As I began the sermon, I looked through the window and saw a bird's nest and the mother feeding the nestlings. Spontaneously, I suggested to the congregation, "You can listen to the sermon or watch the window behind me. That may tell you as much about God."

Neither a wrestling faith nor a nestling faith is the right one. Both are important parts of our relationship with God. Sometimes, as we discover in our grief work, it is necessary and helpful to argue with God, to wrestle with the doubts and questions and anger that we feel at our loss. Sometimes, as we also discover, it is necessary and helpful and comforting to nestle in God, to rest, to be nurtured, to weep and to be cared for.

We are encouraged by Scripture to "not grieve as others do who have no hope" (1 Thess 4:13). Grief is natural and good. But Paul advises that we grieve as people who have hope because God has come to us in God's grace. Sometimes we wrestle with that grace and sometimes we nestle in it, but in all times, God is at work in us. We are at work, like athletes or apprentices learning to master a new trade, becoming people of faith and hope.

The time, reflection, conversation, and prayer we have given to our grief are exercises of faith. These exercises mature and prepare us to affirm life. They have taught us how we are connected to others, to the world, and to God. A loss has an impact on all relationships, and the restoration of hope also impacts and strengthens our relationships.

And as the author points out, to affirm is to pronounce something good. We are affirming even the struggles and pain we have lived, pronouncing them good, and are now moving into the relationships made possible by the honest struggles of our journey.

To Think About

In your own journey through loss and grief, when have you found you have a wrestling faith and when a nestling faith? As you look at these times, what do you think are the benefits of a faith relationship that wrestles and one that nestles?

To Talk About

Have a conversation with a friend about times when you were experiencing a change and easily affirmed the new reality and times when affirming the new thing you were experiencing was more difficult.

To Do

The apostle Paul wrote, "But we do not want you to be uninformed, brothers and sisters, about those who have died, so that you may not grieve as others do who have no hope." Rewrite these words in a way that reflects your own grief journey.

Prayer

Dear God, give me faith and hope so that whether I am wrestling with you or nestling in you, I might always find joy and peace in your presence. In Jesus's name, amen.

AFTERWORD

AS A CHAPLAIN and a professor with joint appointments at the University of Chicago Divinity School and Medical School, our father, Granger Westberg, was expected to preach at Rockefeller Chapel a few times each year. In March 1961, he chose to preach on grief, including the stages many people appeared to go through as they dealt with losing a loved one, a job, or something else that was important in their lives. Many great theologians preached at Rockefeller Chapel, so the Sunday service was broadcast over WGN radio. Typically, the preacher could expect ten to twenty letters from listeners. After Dad preached on grief, he received close to a thousand letters, by far the largest sermon response ever.

Thinking he had suddenly become a noteworthy preacher, Dad worked doubly hard on his next sermon (on a different topic) and preached with great enthusiasm. Ten letters trickled in. Dad realized that it was the topic of grief that had generated the avalanche of letters. Grief was not addressed very much in those days. People were hungry for guidance on how to deal with grief in a healthy way. So Dad expanded on his sermon and wrote *Good Grief.*

Over the decades, almost every time Dad spoke in public, people came up afterward to tell him how much *Good Grief* had helped them during a time of great loss. Pastors, nurses, physicians, funeral directors, and even veterinarians told him that they gave *Good Grief* to patients and clients who were experiencing grief. Dad also received scores of letters of thanks, including one from Mamie Eisenhower. She wrote that after the death of her husband, Ike (President Dwight D. Eisenhower), a friend had given her *Good Grief.* The book, she said, had helped her deal with her loss.

Good Grief has continued to touch people's lives. A likely reason for the book's continued success is the enduring value of Dad's insights and his positive approach to this inevitable part of life. Also, he chose to write a straightforward, easily digestible book, recognizing that when grieving, few people have the energy to delve into a complex book.

Good Grief is indeed accessible. You can look at the table of contents (each chapter being a stage of grief) and think, "Aha! That's me." If you choose, you can skip to that chapter and be assured that what you are experiencing is normal. There is reason for hope.

Dad's message of the relationship between the spirit and health influenced the careers of all of his children. Jane is a medical-school professor who focuses on collaborative, compassionate approaches to medical education and health care. John is a business owner in the death-care industry, working with funeral directors and cemeterians. Joan is a psychiatric social worker who helps families and patients acknowledge their loss and grief when they learn that they must cope with the limitations of mental illness. Jill works in the field of health ministry, most notably with faith communities. We are all indebted to Dad for his insights on living full and healthy lives.

Jane Westberg
Jill Westberg McNamara

Good Grief is indeed accessible. You can look at the table of contents (each chapter being a type of grief) and think, "Aha! That's me." If you choose, you can skip to that chapter and be assured that what you are experiencing is normal. There is reason for hope.

Dad's message of the relationship between the spirit and health influenced the careers of all of his children. Jane is a medical-school professor who focuses on collaborative, compassionate approaches to medical education and health care. John is a business owner in the death-care industry, working with funeral directors and cemeteries. Joan is a psychiatric social worker who helps families and patients acknowledge their loss and grief when they learn that they must cope with the limitations of mental illness. Jill works in the field of health ministry, most notably with faith communities. We are all indebted to Dad for his insights on living full and healthy lives.

Jane Westberg

Jill Westberg McNamara

NOTES

Stage Two: We Express Emotion

1. C. S. Lewis, *A Grief Observed* (New York: HarperOne, 1996), 10.
2. Henri Nouwen, *The Wounded Healer: Ministry in Contemporary Society* (New York: Doubleday, 1979).
3. Chana Bloch, "The Potato Eaters," in *Swimming in the Rain: New and Selected Poems, 1980–2015* (Pittsburgh: Autumn House, 2015).